M000191456

# THE NEW

## *Angel*

## MESSAGES

*Awaken with the Angels*

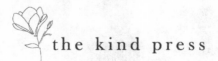
the kind press

# SHUNANDA SCOTT

Copyright © 2022 Shunanda Scott
First published by the kind press, 2022

All rights reserved. No part of this book may be reproduced, stored in a retrieval system
or transmitted in any form or by any means, electronic, mechanical photocopying,
recording, or otherwise, without written permission from the author and publisher.

This publication contains the opinions and ideas of its author. It is intended to provide
helpful and informative material on the subjects addressed in the publication. While the
publisher and author have used their best efforts in preparing this book, the material in
this book is of the nature of general comment only. It is sold with the understanding that
the author and publisher are not engaged in rendering medical advice or any other kind of
personal professional service in the book. In the event that you use any of the information
in this book for yourself, the author and the publisher assume no responsibility for your
actions.

Cover Design: Mila Book Covers
Internal design: Nicola Matthews, Nikki Jane Design
Edited by Georgia Jordan


Cataloguing-in-Publication
entry is available from the
National Library Australia.

NATIONAL
LIBRARY
OF AUSTRALIA

ISBN: 978-0-6450887-0-0
ISBN: 978-0-6450887-1-7 ebook

*For George—*

*Your first breath activated my own awakening
with the Angels.*

# CONTENTS

# Foreword

By Rachelle Sewell

This book is an invitation to journey within your own heart and uncover the true essence that lies within you. Once you've begun, the Angels that guide and support you in your life can gently deliver new insights and experiences to help you blossom into a new version of self. As you read the channelled messages in this book—each encoded with light and healing—they will begin to activate and open your own soul wisdom. What a gift for humanity at this time of transition and change on our planet!

Shunanda Scott's own journey of transformation is openly reflected in the Angelic words of wisdom that flow through each day of *The New Angel Messages*. As you read the light practice techniques, channelled Angel Messages and daily invocations, Shunanda's personal journey becomes a part of your own transition to a higher vibrational experience of beingness.

I recommend dedicating a year of your life to following the messages in the order gifted from the Angels to give yourself the spaciousness of time and the clarity of daily intention to embody each lesson, and increase the depth of your personal transformation.

I have been so profoundly blessed in my own life to have awakened to connection with Angels and Archangels following my first near-death experience at the age of eleven years; the constant flow of wisdom and guidance has completely shaped the events of my life.

Learning to communicate with your Guardian Angels or

asking for support and clarity from Archangels enables you to open to the souls of others and provides comfort, inner resilience, and alignment to life purpose. My Resonate Essences range of vibrational products was gifted from the divine during my second near-death experience, and has supported the ascension of humanity since 2011 and aligned my path with inspirational lightworkers, healers and Angelic messengers.

I am deeply grateful for the synchronicities that guided Shunanda to my private practice in 2010, and am honoured to have been a witness to her personal awakening of communicating with the Angelic realms. She truly embodies her soul mission, sharing her wisdom and intuitive gifts in private practice with clients, with her students through The Angel Aura training programs, and with humanity through this inspirational gift of Angelic co-creation: *The New Angel Messages*. Enjoy this magical journey of awakening.

With love and gratitude,

**Rachelle Sewell xo**
*Channel and co-creator Resonate Essences, advanced kinesiologist, past-life and clinical hypnotherapist, and Life Between Lives Regressionist.*

# *Introduction*

My awakening to the Angels occurred immediately after the birth of my second child. I went to hospital a regular person, somewhat open minded and interested in intuition, but certainly not gifted (and with absolutely no inclination to become an Angel medium). The birth of my son was relatively uneventful in the scheme of things (of course it was pretty momentous for me, and him!). But the night I came home, everything changed. My psychic awareness opened up literally overnight.

It was like a veil had been removed. Suddenly I could hear and feel everything.

I had no idea what was happening, and truthfully, at first, I thought I was imagining things. I remember that first night at home, waking from a deep sleep to hear a conversation in my bedroom. I was so tired in my new-mum daze that I dismissed it as my imagination. However, this phenomenon continued (and increased).

As you can imagine, it was pretty scary for me at the time, and for the first year I suffered panic attacks regularly. I couldn't go to the shops without feeling the emotions and thoughts of everyone around me. I couldn't sleep without being visited by ghosts asking for help, or experiencing psychic attack by unwholesome entities while in a dream state. Navigating this was challenging to say the least, especially with a newborn.

At the beginning of this journey, my experience of intuition was difficult and frightening. I didn't like it! I wanted to turn it off, and I had very little understanding of the Angels. I only began working with Archangel Michael out of desperation as a way to protect myself from the intensity of the empathic and psychic experiences I was having. Over the course of two years, I worked with him every day, shielding myself morning and night in meditation (and sometimes more regularly) to try to lessen the experiences I was having.

I knew there was more to this than just heightened empathic sensitivity. My dreams were coming true regularly, and I was receiving frequent visits from ghosts, so I read and learned everything I could in order to manage this new 'gift'.

Thus, I reluctantly began my Angel journey, more as a way to understand and regulate my abilities than anything else.

Eventually I did an entry-level Angel reader course to try to understand more of what I was experiencing. I was naturally drawn to Angel work as a way to understand my growing psychic abilities, as even then, deep down, I knew it was a safe pathway that would offer unconditional love and protection as I opened up and explored this side of myself.

I nearly didn't pursue this calling. Truthfully, I was very triggered by the religious side of Angel messages. Religion was the antithesis of everything my heart knew to be true about Angels. I didn't resonate with the religious iconography of Angels. Angels didn't look like that to me! The Angels I saw weren't human and did not have a physical body. I also really struggled with how Angels had been presented in the spiritual/New Age community. Regardless of this resistance, something urged me onwards, and so I stumbled blindly and tried to find my own path to working with the Angels.

My life-changing moment came one day in a session with a mentor, who was guiding me through an exercise assisting several ghosts (who had taken up residence in my house) back to the light. During this session, I had my most profound Angel experience to date. I will never forget the intense bliss, tears of joy, and heart-cracking love that I experienced as each soul—under the guardianship of Archangel Michael and Archangel Azrael—journeyed to the light and was reunited with family. Nor will I forget the indescribable love I felt as the Angels helped me to facilitate this reunion. The love I felt was like nothing I knew from my earthly experience, but it felt familiar in my heart.

Back then, I often found it hard to connect with the Angels. My ability to connect was sporadic and intermittent. I didn't trust myself. I couldn't tell what was my imagination, and what was a real Angel message. Sometimes I would have an easy spontaneous connection; other times, especially when I really needed their guidance, they would be silent. I often felt frustrated and blocked.

Sometimes when I would open to connect, I would be inundated with ghosts and dark entities also connecting with me. Eek! This wasn't fun AT ALL. I had two young children, and—little did I know it—was about to fall pregnant with my third.

I took more courses and read more books, I practised, I meditated, I journaled. I received valuable mentoring from trusted sacred guides who taught me how to manage and use my newly opened intuitive abilities, and how to do it safely. I practised some more.

Over time, I became more confident at recognising the communication of the Angels, and more comfortable receiving and decoding their messages. Eventually, I was guided to fly to New York to do an advanced Angel teacher training course.

This was my next mission activation, and after that trip, the Angels took over. From that point onwards, all my Angel training has been received directly from the Angels (however, I have always had a mentor to support me as I develop and recommend you do too).

***

I dreamed about this book. I saw the title in a dream, and even though I had no idea of how this journey would play out, I knew as I woke that it was important. At the time, I didn't know it was a book. In fact, I thought it was an oracle card deck!

It took a few years for the journey of the New Angel Messages to crystallise and take shape. I tried to force the journey, and eventually gave up, thinking it wasn't to be. Then one day, when I was least expecting it, the Angels tapped me on the shoulder and told me to stop what I was doing. Literally. At the time, I was very close to burnout. I had been stuck in a challenging work role that involved lots of travel for little reward, and it was taking a huge toll on me as a single parent. The Angels very clearly asked me to take some time out from the work that had been consuming me. They asked me to trust them. So, I did.

Over the next six months, I stopped, and listened. I spent time in nature, I journaled, I meditated. It required constant leaps of faith and was one of the most intense energetic experiences of my life. Some days, I could literally feel the energy coursing through me as the Angels prepared me physically and energetically for the experience of receiving the New Angel Messages. Nature and the ocean were my saviours, where I often spent hours each day integrating this powerful frequency upgrade.

Little did I know it, but this was my next (and most potent) sacred mission activation. Every step to that point had been guided by the Angels. Every step during that journey felt like a massive leap of faith. Every step asked me to surrender, let go, and trust their vision and messages. Every step was to prepare me for what was to come.

In the midst of this process, while out on a horse ride, I was struck dumb (literally motionless), when Archangel Butyalil came through unexpectedly and spoke to me. It's rare that the Angels interrupt me without warning, and yet there he was, out there in the sunshine with glorious parklands all around, specifically asking me to start writing the New Angel Messages. It felt like time stood still in that moment; it was so powerful, loving energy was emanating all through me. Just like my first life-changing Angel experience, I burst into instant tears of blissful joy.

My experience intensified from that moment onwards, and shortly afterwards, the Angels guided me to visit Uluru to receive my next steps. 'Ok! When?' I asked. *Next week*, they said. So off I went. Whilst walking the ten-kilometre base track around this incredibly powerful sacred site, the Angels gave me their plan. They asked me to commit to channelling a message from them every day for a year. *Every day?* I thought. *Really?* What could they possibly have to say that was so important that I needed to commit to every day? Would I run out of messages?

By now, I trusted the Angels enough to know that I would be supported, even if I didn't understand the full purpose of this journey (I still didn't even realise that this was going to be the book). So I took another leap of faith, and made a public announcement on my social media committing to share the messages with my audience, every day, for a year. (Truthfully, I was a little terrified of this commitment, so the public announcement also kept me accountable.)

It wasn't until a few months into this experience of channelling the New Angel Messages that I began to understand what was happening, and why they had intervened. This was about the great awakening! The Angels had interrupted me at the exact right time. They had stopped everything in my life to prepare me for my mission: to bring the New Angel Messages to the world at the time when we most needed their support.

Over the course of the year, I shared the New Angel Messages every single day. I didn't ask for them, I just showed up. The messages came through at different times of the day, whenever I felt their nudge (and sometimes whenever I could make the time … remember, I'm also a single mumma of three children). It truly was a complete act of faith on my part. Nothing was planned. Not once did I know before the moment of writing what they wanted to share. I didn't know their intent, and it took me about four months to realise and fully trust that they had a big-picture plan all along.

Midway through this journey, I realised something else was happening.

As I received and channelled the messages each day, I was experiencing my own personal shift. The messages were changing me! They were taking me even deeper in my own Angel relationship, deeper in my faith, deeper in my understanding of myself and the divine than I thought was possible. My own experience of awakening was being shaped by the messages I was channelling each day. My relationships, consciousness, sense of self, and sense of the changing world around me was being extended and challenged by the messages as they came through.

By the end of the year, I could see that the Angels had taken both me and my audience along on a powerful journey of transformation and awakening.

I was also receiving countless messages every day from people sharing their gratitude and thanks, saying how much the New Angel Messages had assisted them through their own awakening.

Now that the process is complete, I am able to reflect on my personal experience.

I feel changed as a result of this process. I feel calmer, more at peace, more confident, and more connected to the divine. My intuition has increased exponentially (which I didn't think was even possible). I feel far less attached to challenging personal circumstances and global situations (which blows me away given the rapid change occurring in the world now). My faith in myself and in the Angels is deeper than ever. I feel confident and powerful even through life's challenges and have a stronger sense of who I am than ever before. On tough days, I have a strong

Angel practice to support me with powerful and loving guidance. I feel more able to see the big picture for myself and the world and have a strong sense of hope and excitement for our future.

One of the most significant shifts for me is that I am no longer afraid. After years of working with the Angels, I now know that I am eternal, that I have both family members and Angels waiting for me when it is my time to return to the light. I do not fear death. I believe in miracles; I see them every day. Despite my initial (and ongoing) religious resistance, I have found my own pathway to the Angels, and by extension, to the infinite one creator/God/source.

There is no one word or phrase that I've found that encompasses the enormity of the loving consciousness that Angels are a part of. The consciousness that you, I and every being are a part of.

I fumble when I try to describe this consciousness. It just feels so big that words don't do it justice. The word God seems so limited when trying to explain something that encompasses so much love, so much potential, so much infinite creation energy and possibility. The Angels helped me find, trust and open to this source of infinite love.

I was initially a reluctant Angel medium. I didn't consciously choose this pathway. It chose me.

Now? I wouldn't change a thing. Sharing the New Messages from the Angels is my mission and has changed me in ways I could not ever have imagined.

Today, *you* begin your awakening with the Angels, and it is my absolute honour to witness and support you on this journey, as your sacred guide.

# PART I

# Awakening with the Angels

# Introduction to the Angels

I am not religious. I have strong feelings about mainstream religion, specifically the Catholic Church with its massive wealth and history of sexual abuse of children. I could never get my head around a religion that included rituals of eating the body of Christ and blood of Christ. I could never reconcile the seemingly obvious hypocrisy of their immense wealth while so much of the world is in poverty. It made no sense to me that the Angels were connected with a religion that was entrenched with shame, corruption, fear and judgement (this goes against everything I understand about Angels). In my heart, I knew everyone could commune directly with the divine, not just those in positions of religious power. As a result, it was challenging for me to begin working with the Angels. I felt a real resistance to this journey on a deep level.

I also discovered that there is a belief among some religions that channelling is the work of the devil. This made no sense and went against everything I knew to be true from my direct experiences communicating with the Angels. My experiences had been blissful! Healing! Life changing. Life affirming. The Angels have never made me feel afraid, ashamed, or abandoned. They have instead, in every instance, offered me complete unconditional love and acceptance. I have never felt like I required their forgiveness or felt any judgement. This felt exactly like what I knew the divine to be, in my heart, and confirmed my suspicions about the hypocrisy and darkness I could see and feel in some aspects of mainstream religion.

Let me be one-hundred-per-cent clear: Angels have NOTHING to do with religion.

Religion, for the most part, is a construct of the false light matrix. It is filled with incredible evil and darkness, which is now being exposed for all to see as the veil crumbles.

Yes, Angels appear in religious texts, but many of the messages from the Angels within such texts are distorted and have been corrupted and used for the dark agenda of religion. Angels were here before religion existed. Angels will be here after religion is exposed as the control mechanism that it is.

Any religious Angel teaching that includes fear, judgement, shame, external authority, or power over you is not a clear Angel message.

There are very few clear Angel channels in the world, and unfortunately, many distortions.

It is my mission to correct this and be a clear channel for the New Angel Messages to come into the world. It is also my mission to teach (and remind) YOU how to speak with the Angels (for we all have this memory and ability within us just as surely as we can speak and breathe).

You don't need me, a priest, a guru or any other intermediary to speak with the Angels. It is your sovereign birth right.

Everyone can learn to speak with the Angels.

Everyone has Angels.

It is completely, one-hundred-per-cent safe for you to begin learning to speak with the Angels, and in this book, you will learn how.

Channelling is *not* the work of the devil. Far from it. Channelling is a form of communication, as natural as speaking, that we all can master (although, like every skill, some find it easier than others). Channelling is a high-level form of intuition that uses energy to communicate. A trained and skilled channel can communicate with Angels as easily as speaking. This is sometimes called an Angel Medium, or Angel Messenger.

In this book, it is my intention to guide you safely through the process of remembering how to speak with Angels, so that you may experience the incredible love, acceptance and hope from the Angels that has changed my life, and the lives of my students and clients.

## What are Angels?

Angels are high-frequency light beings that serve the infinite creator (God, or source). Angels are ninth-density (9D) frequency or higher, and have no physical form. Angels are not human. Unlike most religious (and many spiritual) depictions, Angels do not have a human-like appearance. Instead, they have an energy field, or aura. Guardian Angels have a golden auric field, and Archangels have a pure white field with different colours at the edges.

Angels communicate with humans via energy, which—as energetic beings—we are able to understand and decode using our intuition (Clairsentience, Claircognicence, Clairaudience and Clairvoyance).

There are infinite numbers of Angels, but there are specific Angels who are assisting us now.

## Guardian Angels

Guardian Angels are different from Archangels. Every human has a minimum of two Guardian Angels assigned to us (some starseeds and lightworkers have as many as four). Guardian Angels are with us before we incarnate, during every second of our earthly journey, and after we transition back to the light/source/Heaven. Guardian Angels hold a 9D frequency. Our loved ones who cross back to the light are not, and do not, become our Guardian Angels. Loved ones can and do visit with messages and guidance occasionally, but Angelic guardianship is a specific and sacred role performed only by the Guardian Angels.

## Archangels

Archangels exist at tenth density (10D) frequency. There are infinite Archangels, but there are currently a specific group assist the human experience. Archangels have a broader overseeing role and focus on specific themes and areas to assist humanity. We can work with Archangels at any time, but they support us in a different way from our personal Guardian Angels.

## What do Angels look and feel like?

Angels are not human. It is very common, when starting out, for our mind to assign a human face and characteristics to our Angels when we meet them in meditation (especially since most literature and images have depicted them this way). I did. You may have also. However, as you progress, your Angels will reveal their true form to you when you are ready.

Angels are an iridescent aura of energy and light. Imagine a human shape, now take away the body and see only light, as radiant, and white as the sun. Now imagine that light surrounded by a glow of the northern lights. This is what an Angel looks like to me in my third-eye communication, and it's even more magnificent when you see them with your physical eyes.

Angels also arrive with an intense energy of pure, unconditional love, acceptance, and bliss. You will *never* mistake the arrival of an Angel in meditation. Sometimes it's subtle, a gentle, warm glow enveloping your heart—sensations of energy and love beginning to move through you and awaken you to their incoming energy and presence. Other times it's intense and instant. The Angels will work with you at your pace. They don't appear fully at first, as truthfully, this would probably be a bit of a shock. They reveal themselves slowly, at your comfort level and at your level of invitation.

The first time I fully connected with Archangel Michael, I burst into tears of joy. The love I felt was so overpowering and pure. This still happens regularly, and it's taken years of practice for me to *not* cry during client Angel readings. With time and practice, you will instantly recognise the arrival of the Angels.

There are thirty-five Angels that have asked to work with you on this journey, and they are listed in the reference section.

These are the thirty-five Angels guiding humanity now.

You will see that through the journey, these Angels have come through in the messages with invitations to work with them on a deeper level.

### What is ascension?

*Ascension: the process of intentionally raising your vibration and expanding your consciousness via the human experience. Ascension is realised over many lifetimes, with the ultimate goal of ascending, or no longer incarnating in physical form.*

There is a direct correlation between your vibration and your ability to connect with your Angels.

There is a direct correlation between your vibration and your capacity to love.

You are an energetic being. You are literally created from love, and an expression of love. Love is the pathway and answer to everything that you seek. Love is the fabric of the universe, and love is consciousness.

Angels are love.

The journey of connecting with the Angels is a journey of exploring love.

Love, and actions chosen with loving intent, raise your vibration and bring you into a higher frequency.

The higher your frequency, the easier it is to connect with and hear and feel your Angels.

The more you love yourself and your life, the more your daily actions are chosen with love at their core, the more your frequency rises, the more you heal yourself, the more authentic your expression of self and life becomes, and the easier it becomes to feel and hear your Angels.

The journey of raising your vibration is sometimes called the ascension journey.

This journey is more than just learning to speak with Angels.

It is a discovery of self, a reconnection with infinite love, a healing, a release of karmic wounds, a discovery of your mission and purpose, and a realisation of your infinite magnificence.

Ascension is just a word. This journey is about opening your heart and exploring love through your human relationships, experiences, and lessons.

The Angels are the guide and mirror on this journey of reclaiming love.

# How to use this book

Everyone can learn to speak with Angels, and this book will take you on a deep immersive journey of learning and remembering how to speak with your Angels.

The New Angel Messages are designed to be read one day at a time, in sequence, over a year.

The messages are powerful, loving, and energetic, and will activate, extend and support you through your own sacred awakening. This process is also known as 'ascension'.

The messages were channelled as an anchor point through powerful times of transformation, both within and without.

The messages will assist you both through your personal life experience and through your understanding of the collective experience. No matter what is happening in the world, or when you are reading this book, they are for you.

Today is the beginning of a sacred journey, and you are now being guided and held by the Angels.

You need not force this. As you read this book, and bring your awareness to the messages each day, and when guided implement the practices below, your ability to speak with Angels will gradually open up all on its own.

You can read this book start to finish in one sitting, but to get the most out of the messages, I suggest you then re-read them in order, one per day, over a year. Once you've completed this process, you can use the messages as an oracle, opening to any page when you need guidance.

*Each day, over twelve months, read one Angel message,*
*in sequence from start to finish. Start on the day that suits*
*you. Start today.*

## Your Angel Practice:

Learning to speak with Angels takes practice.

Your practice need not be perfect; all it needs to be is regular.

Don't overcomplicate this … you don't need any fancy rituals
or special feathers. You don't need to speak out loud to talk with
your Angels.

Allow yourself ten minutes. Have a journal ready (your phone
is fine). Take a quiet moment, centre yourself, close your eyes,
and in your mind say the following:

*Angels, I invite you to work with me.*

Then read the day's message.

Remember, each message contains light codes and frequencies
of the infinite love of the creator/source/God. Each message is
designed by the Angels to take you on a journey, a journey that is
perfect for you in this moment.

Practise detachment and let go of expectations. Some messages
will move you instantly. Some will sit gently and make you
curious. Some will only make sense after some time has passed.
The full experience will only be understood after completion of
the 365 days.

Make a short record in your journal of any feelings or
responses that come up for you. Not all messages will be for you.
Not all parts of the message will be for you. Journal whatever feels
natural and spontaneous for you in that moment.

# Advanced Practice #1

**Your Angel Practice:**

If you are experiencing a challenge, you can ask your Angels for further guidance.

The quality of the question you ask has a direct impact on the way the Angels will respond.

Before you begin, remember, Angels are bound to respect your free will, so will always answer in a way that will not scare you nor violate the miracle of your earthly experience.

Angel messages always feel loving, compassionate, and empowering.

Over time, with a daily Angel practice, you will notice that answers flow automatically after you ask questions.

At first, you might feel as if it's your imagination, or that you are making it up. Write it down anyway.

With time, you will be able to discern the subtle whispers of an Angel message, which are very different from your own mind and from your ego.

**Questions to ask the Angels**

- *What is my highest priority today?*
- *What messages do you have for me today?*
- *What am I missing in this situation?*
- *Please show me what I cannot see?*
- *Is it the right time to take action?*

Remember, this is a leap of faith. Miracles will occur as part of this journey. You WILL be changed by the end of the process. Set no intentions other than to be open to the journey that is meant for you.

# Advanced practice #2

## Your Light Practice

What is a light practice? When I began working with the Angels in earnest, they guided me to develop my own unique daily practice, with the intention of raising my vibration.

*Your light practice is anything that raises your vibration.*

The benefits of having a daily light practice are multiple and have completely transformed my life.

Your light practice is any activity that changes your energy, your mood, or your vibration.

Your light practice is anything that heals you.

Your light practice is anything that brings clarity and visibility or LIGHT to your life.

Your light practice is anything that brings love, joy and light into your mind, body, and spirit.

Your light practice is anything that you love!

Over time, with daily implementation, your light practice will be the most important foundation for your awakening and ascension journey.

## Benefits of having a daily Light Practice

- A stronger vibration and stronger energetic boundaries (less psychic attack, less energetic vampirism, less empathic sensitivity)
- Feeling strong, vibrant, and powerful
- An increase in intuition (yes, there is a direct correlation)
- An increase in your ability to speak with and hear your Angels
- Intense feelings of love, happiness, and joy
- Increased physical vitality and strength

- Increased sense of self-worth

My personal light practice has shifted and changed over the years. I suggest you start with what is easy, affordable, and accessible for you right now. You will be guided to shift and adjust your light practice as you shift, grow and change.

### Discovering your light practice

In your journal, write a list of all the activities that bring instant feelings of love, light and joy into your being. Don't worry too much about whether you can afford them, or whether you have time for them. Just write them down anyway.

Some examples of my light practice and my students' light practice include: Watching the sun rise, using essential oils, having a nap, meditation, watching a comedy, reading, swimming in the ocean, moving your body in ways that feel good, sex/self-pleasure, creativity, spending time in nature, getting a massage, etc.

The one activity that the Angels insist on as part of your light practice is spending time in nature. This raises your vibration more than any other practice and has a multitude of other benefits too. At times I have been guided to spend several hours a day in nature (often when I am sick, under stress, or experiencing a significant life challenge). This is when it seems impossible to create that amount of time, and yet when I have, this has been the single most powerful support when I've needed it most.

## Advanced practice #3

You can work closely with the specific Archangels who assisted with the process of the New Angel Messages (you can find the page references for each Archangel lesson in the reference section on pg. 419). You can do this by intentionally connecting with the invocation for the specific Angel when you feel guided and exploring your growing relationship with them.

Keep a journal and record any messages or shifts in awareness that come up along this journey as a record to look back on.

### Frequently asked questions:

- What do Angel messages feel like?
  When you are communicating with the Angels it will always feel safe, loving, and empowering. Angels will never scare you, judge you, laugh at you, talk down to you, be angry with you, or judge you. Angels will never violate your free will, shame you, or speak to your ego voice. These are the core rules to follow to identify if you are speaking with an Angelic being. If the message you are receiving doesn't adhere to the above, it's not Angelic.
- How do I know if I'm speaking with my Angels, or if it's my imagination?
  Angels have a different tone and sentence structure with their communication and offer a higher point of reference to our own mind and awareness. There is a neutrality and softness to their dialogue that is filled with compassion and acceptance. With time, trust, and regular practice this will become easily discernible from your own inner voice.
- What are the most common ways Angels communicate

with us?

Angels communicate in ways we can easily recognise, and its different for every individual. You will use your four intuitive "clairs" (Clairvoyance, Clairsentience, Clairaudience, and Claircognisance) to translate and decode their messages. Your Angels always know exactly how to communicate with you in a way that you will understand.

Clairvoyant Angel messages: initially these will be visual signs in your day. Feathers, coins, repeated numbers, rainbows etc. These will then progress to images that you see in your mind's eye during a meditation or a lucid dream state. With practice you will be able to see visions in your mind as if replaying a scene from a movie. When you are ready, you may even begin to see Angels with your physical eyes. It took me 11 years before I saw my first Angel in real life (it was a truly incredible experience, and SO worth the wait!).

Clairsentient Angel messages: are received as goosebumps, shivers, energetic jolts, emotions, and sensations of energy moving through your body. All "empaths" have very strong natural clairsentient abilities. Learning to master this form or energetic communication and discern and protect yourself from external energies can be life changing for sensitive empaths. Clairsentience is my strongest intuitive ability, and mastering it was life changing for me.

Clairaudient Angel messages: initially this is external, most commonly through music lyrics. Then you will progress to hearing spoken messages in your mind as if you are recalling a conversation. With practice you will be able to converse with them in a meditation, or even hear sentences in your mind as you go about your day.

Advanced clairaudience is also known as channelling and is a highly skilled form of telepathic communication. Claircognisant Angel messages: strong feelings of instant knowing that come to you from nowhere. Men often have naturally developed Claircognicence, and "just know" what to do.

An advanced Angel student or Angel Messenger will use all four "clairs" and combine the four message streams into one complete message. This takes time, practice, and training. My Angel Messenger Certification teaches students how to channel Angel Messages at this advanced level.

- I feel blocked: how can I have a deeper connection with my Angels?

  Everyone can learn/remember to speak with Angels. You are not blocked, you are learning, and with practice you can and will develop your skills. My Angel Immersion course teaches you how to speak with Angels and develop your confidence and skills so you can learn to speak with the Angels directly, without the need for a medium.

**For more support:**

During this journey, you may feel guided to go deeper with your awakening with the Angels.

Here are the next steps I recommend, and how you can work with me:

1. Join my sacred light community, The Angel Aura, where I channel weekly written Angel Transmissions, and hold fortnightly live channelled Angel Transmissions with the Angels. This space is for all starseeds and lightworkers on their ascension journey and will rapidly accelerate your

awakening with the Angels.

2. Enrol in my Angel Immersion course, which is designed for beginner to intermediate Angel students. The Angel Immersion course will teach you the core foundations of working with Angels, as well as developing a strong Light Practice and Angel practice.

3. Enrol in my Angel Messenger Certification to learn how to channel Angel Messages professionally as a qualified Angel Messenger. This course is for all Angel Immersion students ready to train with me at practitioner level and runs for four months in an online group setting.

**Resources:**

Here are some free resources to help you get started on your awakening with the Angels:

**Angel Practice PDF**
https://www.shunanda.co/wp-content/uploads/2020/04/Dear-Angels-The-Angel-Immersion-Shunanda-PRINT.pdf

**Light Practice PDF**
https://www.shunanda.co/wp-content/uploads/2020/04/My-Light-Practice-The-Angel-Immersion-Shunanda-PRINT.pdf

**Mini Angel Guide**
https://www.shunanda.co/wp-content/uploads/2021/03/Mini-Angel-Guide-Shunanda2.pdf

**Guardian Angel Meditation**
https://www.shunanda.co/wp-content/uploads/2017/11/Lady-Gaia-Meditation-Activate-Your-Lightworker-Power.mp3

## Community support:

- Join the New Angel Messages FREE Facebook
  community:
  This is a free space where I share my channelled Angel
  messages, and a great starting point for your awakening
  with the Angels.
  facebook.com/groups/new.angel.messages
- Join the Angel Aura (exclusive membership):
  The Angel Aura community is a private membership
  space and an affordable next step to deepen your Angel
  relationship. In the Angel Aura you will receive powerful
  weekly written Angel Transmissions and can join
  fortnightly live Angel Transmissions held on zoom. You
  will also be able to connect with our amazing community
  of fellow Lightworkers and Starseeds from all over the
  world.
  angelaura.co

# PART II

# *The new Angel Messages*

Today begins the journey of your awakening with the Angels. We are moving through a significant time of change for humanity. A complete shift in consciousness, and the dawning of a new age. The Angels want to speak with you. They want you to know that you need not go through this journey alone. There are many misunderstandings and misconceptions about working with Angels. And there are new messages and new Angels, here to support us through changing times.

# DAY 1

*Angel lesson: Guardian Angels*

Welcome to day one of your awakening with the Angels. Today, you will meet your Guardian Angels.

We all have Guardian Angels. They are with us from before we incarnate, until we pass back to the light. Think of them as your personal squad. They are your best friends, your therapist, your sibling, your parent, your life coach, and your mentor.

They know everything about you (but don't worry, they don't pry or spy). They know you better than you know yourself.

They are always loving, forgiving and completely, one-hundred-per-cent accepting of every decision you make. They will never laugh at you, belittle you, shame you or be angry with you. *Ever.*

They love you with a fierceness and depth that is so big that if you fully opened to it, you'd burst into tears. And you will.

You know their language, and they know yours! Today they want to assure you that they know exactly how to get messages through to you, and of course they know exactly what you need to hear (remember, it's rarely what we think we need).

I don't have a special gift as an Angel medium. You can do what I do. I've practised, practised more, and spent years mastering my craft. And you can too.

——————— Angel practice ———————

Please spend a few minutes centring and connecting with your Guardian Angels now. You might like to use my free meditation (pg. 16), and the invocation below.

*Angels, I invite you to work with me now. Please assist me on this journey of connecting with you, as I open my heart to feel and receive your loving guidance. Please give me clear messages that I will easily feel, see, hear, and understand.*

**Guiding Angels: Guardian Angels**
**Energy: Masculine or Feminine**
**Aura colour: Golden**

# DAY 2

## *Channelled Angel message*

We are always with you.

You don't need a complicated ritual to speak with us.

You can speak with us in your mind.

You can speak with us as you go about your day.

You can speak with us when you're driving.

You can speak with us in public.

You can speak with us in private.

You can speak with us in meditation, in prayer, in nature, and whenever or wherever you want to.

We are never busy. Time and space do not exist as you know them, and so we are able to be with you the instant you call on us.

We are never tired of hearing from you.

We will never ignore you. Ever.

If you are going through a challenging time, and you need to call on us hourly for reassurance, then we will be there every single time you ask.

We want you to feel safe. We want you to feel loved and know that you are never truly alone.

As you work with us, we will assist you through the process of gently identifying any blocks, veils, beliefs, or walls that have prevented you from feeling and hearing our loving guidance, and from feeling and experiencing love.

Speaking with us is something that you can learn and remember as easily as any other task you have attempted.

In time, it will feel as natural as breathing.

*We look forward to working with you!*

—————— Invocation ——————

*Angels, I am ready to let go of my beliefs and veils so I may feel and hear your presence and feel and experience love.*

**Guiding Angels:  All Angels**

# DAY 3

*Channelled Angel message*

When you are experiencing life's most difficult challenges, it is natural to question why the event is happening.

We want you to know that our guidance will assist you on the most challenging days. You need not face life's darkest hours alone.

Even in the midst of seemingly insurmountable challenges, we are with you.

We want you to know that life is an experience of *all* aspects of the human adventure. This is a full-spectrum experience. We remind you that when you incarnated, you consciously chose to participate in the full, rich, and diverse experience as a human.

You are not meant to have a perfect life. Permanent happiness and perfection are not the goal of life. All emotions are ok. All experiences are important. All experiences are chosen.

We offer you an invitation to soften and allow yourself to be more accepting of the darkness and so-called 'negative' life experiences, because they are an essential part of the magnificent, rich tapestry of the full human experience.

In the depths of grief, you can experience miraculous understanding about love.

In the depths of sorrow, you can gain a miraculous perspective on joy.

In the depths of physical pain, you can experience the wonders of healing, and find incredible passion and purpose in helping others in similar circumstances.

We are with you always and will assist you to find a peaceful pathway on your journey, and help you feel less alone as you experience the hardest and darkest challenges of your life.

—————— Invocation ——————

*Angels, please remind me that there is a purpose and reason for all life's experiences. Please help me feel strong and resilient to move through challenging days.*

**Guiding Angels:**
**Archangel Faith, Archangel Raphael, Archangel Zadkiel**

# DAY 4
*Channelled Angel message*

There is a profound period of change currently underway on Earth.

This has already begun and will continue for many years.

In your heart, you know this to be true. You can see the

change occurring externally and are experiencing your own inner transformation and change.

At times, it may feel as if you are experiencing increased sensitivity, heightened emotions, exploration of identity, and transformational change. You are drawn to self-healing, and yet also experience pain and heartbreak at the state of the world.

We are here to help you through this experience of change, awakening and ascension.

We want so much to work with you to support you, as your transformation and healing are intrinsically linked with the earth's transformation and healing.

We can guide you every step of the way through your own healing and ascension journey. We will support you as you heal.

We love you! You are not alone!

You are ready now to work with us.

You already know and feel our language, as it is the language of energy and love.

You are worthy, deserving, and ready.

─────── Invocation ───────

*Angels, I am ready to begin my journey of connecting with you. Please guide me with clear messages that I can easily hear, see, and understand.*

**Guiding Angels:**
**Archangel Haniel, Archangel Nathaniel, Archangel Metatron**

# DAY 5

*Channelled Angel message*

We accept and love you unconditionally, in all your uniqueness.

You are meant to be you. A fully expressed, uncensored, liberated, joyful expression of your unique self!

There are many rules and beliefs within the collective that shape your experience. They are not true, and they are not you. These filters can often limit you and hold you back. Many humans live much of their life filtered through these rules and beliefs.

The awakening journey is the beginning of the removal of these veils, and the discovery of the true you.

We will guide you on this journey, and we love you unconditionally.

We encourage you to begin a curious self-examination of where your own rules and beliefs are holding you back right now.

Where are you not expressing all parts of yourself?

Where are you dimming your light, hiding your beauty, softening your opinions, not speaking up, containing your emotions, hiding your anger, or taking the safest choice possible?

We would love to see you open to a rebellious, playful, joyful, and passionate exploration of your full human experience!

For you are meant to be YOU in all your glory!

We hold no judgement over your choices. There is no judgement day. There is only self-judgement, and self-acceptance.

As long as your actions do not harm another and are made from a place of love and joyful expression of self, then we encourage you to freely and with abandon express *all* parts of yourself!

Let this notion be with you during your journey with us, and onwards. Let yourself be curious and compassionate, playful, and explorative, creative, and childlike in your journey of expressing YOU in all your true, unhidden radiance.

——————— Invocation ———————

*Angels, help me gently discover my inner, hidden heart and radiance. Help me identify veils, blocks, and beliefs, and gently let them go when they no longer serve me.*

**Guiding Angels:**
**Archangel Nathaniel, Archangel Metatron**

# DAY 6

## Channelled Angel message

There is nothing to be afraid of. Even when challenging things are happening, most of the time it is never as bad as it seems, and afterwards there is often a profound gift, lesson, or silver lining in the experience.

Things will always turn out ok. In fact, often, they will turn out far better than you can imagine. It is easy to imagine the worst-case scenario is the most likely outcome. We want to assure you that the universe is life affirming, and in fact the worst-case scenario is actually the *least* likely outcome.

There is always a positive side to every difficult experience. There is no light without shade.

There is magic and mystery to life, and there are twists and turns, and bumps and bruises.

However, we want you to know that even in the worst scenarios, death is not the end.

You are an eternal being.

There is nothing to fear in death.

Death is not an ending, rather it is a new beginning, and you are welcomed home with love, joy, healing, acceptance, and celebration.

Accepting that there will always be difficult parts to life is the first step towards feeling less fear and welcoming in more love.

Accepting that you need not fear death is transformational.

We can help you with this. We can also help you find support if you need it, via a healer, sacred guide, or friend.

**Note from Shunanda**

Archangel Michael can help you feel safe and protected, and help you process fearful situations or feelings. He can help you identify whether the feelings are yours, or whether you are tuning into a collective fear, or empathically picking up on the fear of another. He can help you clear any fearful energy from your vibration, and he can help you protect your aura and raise your vibration.

Working with the Angels over time will result in you feeling more peace and less fear. You will no longer fear death, and you will feel more acceptance about the ups and downs (or light and dark) aspects of your life.

Nothing will change, except your perspective and how you feel about life. So, in some ways, everything will change.

———— Invocation ————

*Angels, please help me let go of fear. Please help me realise that I am safe, that I am supported, and able to open to a peaceful and loving experience of life.*

**Guiding Angels:**
**Archangel Michael, Archangel Azrael, Archangel Faith**

# DAY 7

*Angel lesson: Archangel Raphael*

Angels feel like love. You may not 'see' them in your mind's eye at first, but you will most certainly feel their presence.

When you are going through an intense physical healing

experience, you can lessen the intensity by working with Archangel Raphael on a regular basis.

Archangel Raphael will only ever give you as much healing light as you are ready to receive.

You will feel intense love wash all through you when you work with him. You may also feel energy pulsing through different parts of your body as you visualise the light pouring through you.

Sometimes you will feel instant emotional relief. Other times you will feel instantly more energised. Or you may feel tired and need to rest to let the light continue to integrate.

Archangel Raphael will also help you find the right healer to assist you with your physical healing journey.

You do not need to be religious to work with Archangel Raphael.

There is no danger in working with Archangels. They will never do anything that would harm you in any way or go against your free will.

They do need your permission to help, so please remember to ask.

———— Angel practice ————

Sit comfortably or lie down in a quiet space.
Close your eyes, draw your attention within.
Soften your body and relax your breathing.
Now imagine your crown chakra (at the top of your head) softening and opening. Visualise a stream of pure emerald light from source entering your crown chakra, pouring slowly down through each of your chakras, and spreading outwards through your physical body. Continue until the emerald light has encompassed every part of your body.
Imagine the light now extending and emanating around you, like a ball of radiant emerald healing light.
Allow yourself to be present in this healing light for as long as you feel guided.

*Archangel Raphael, I invite you to work with me now. Please surround my whole body with pure emerald healing light. Please remind me that I am able to heal, that I am whole, that I am my healer, that I am healing.*

**Guiding Angel: Archangel Raphael**
**Energy: Masculine**
**Aura colour: Brilliant Emerald green**

# DAY 8

## *Channelled Angel message*

You are safe to open your heart.

In fact, we encourage you to not only practise this, but welcome it.

You cannot explore the full human experience with a closed heart.

With a closed and protected heart, you will experience a filtered and limited version of love, joy, trust, empathy, friendship, and all the wonderful learning experiences that come through the magic of human interaction.

With a closed heart, you will find it harder to connect with the divine, to use your powerful intuition, and to love others freely.

We will assist you on this tender and sacred journey.

You are safe to give and receive love through your radiant, open, and powerfully loving heart.

### Note from Shunanda

The Archangel to work with to begin to open your heart chakra is Archangel Raphael.

You can do this slowly. As you begin to open your heart, you will immediately notice that all your feelings feel more intense. You may experience waves of joy, followed by waves of sorrow.

You may also notice that you feel intense amounts of love for all the people already in your life.

You may notice that you feel closer and more connected to nature and animals.

You may also notice that you feel the need to release old grief that you may have stored away from past painful experiences.

Opening your heart is a slow, tender, and sacred journey. Call on Archangel Raphael to regularly send healing light to your heart chakra and be open to the support of a professional such as a counsellor or therapist if you feel you need it. Ask your Guardian Angels to help you find the right person for you.

———————— Invocation ————————

*Archangel Raphael, please help me to gently open my heart chakra, and express any emotions and feelings that have been held within its protective walls. Please help me feel safe as I gently open to a deeper experience of love.*

**Guiding Angels: Archangel Raphael**

# DAY 9

*Angel lesson: Guardian Angels*

My main Guardian Angel's name is Peter. He is cheeky and playful, makes me sing songs to clients in readings, and encourages me to swear. (When I'm feeling passionate about something, and feeling unguarded, I often swear. This is a part of myself when I'm completely ME, and Archangel Peter always encourages me to let go of my walls.)

He often makes jokes during very serious moments, and this

helps me drop out of my head, and into my heart.

There is a myth about Angels being serious and sombre. It's not true. In fact, sometimes Angels are HILARIOUS! And they love nothing more than to see us laughing, being playful, and expressing this side of ourselves.

We are all spiritual beings. There is no hierarchy and no judgement on this journey.

We are all spiritual because we are all human.

Now that's clear, I encourage you to have a little more fun with your Angel practice, and with our communication with our Angels!

——————— Invocation ———————

*Angels, please show me how I can have more joy in my life. Please guide me to activities that will help me express humour, play and fun.*

**Guiding Angels: Archangel Jophiel, Guardian Angels**

# DAY 10

## Angel lesson: Angel communication

On some level, you already know how to speak Angel language.

Learning to speak with Angels is something we can all do. It's not for a select few. It's not a special gift.

Angels speak the language of love.

Learning Angel language requires belief, trust, an open heart.

It is not what you expect, and you will need to unlearn everything you think you know.

Your Angels will always speak to you in the way they know you will understand.

Some common ways Angels speak with you are:

- Signs in nature, like butterflies, love hearts, and rainbows
- Music, like song lyrics that have particular meaning coming on at just the right time (a form of clairaudience)
- Instant gut feelings of 'knowing' (Claircognicence)
- Automatic writing (which can be practised as a journaling exercise)
- Intense energetic waves of love flooding through your heart and body (clairsentience)
- Messages that you hear in your mind, similar to recalling a conversation (clairaudience)
- Visions that you see either with your eyes or in your mind (clairvoyance)
- Messages from strangers or friends at the exact right time
- Signs that appear online, on television or on social media
- Unusual coincidences
- Messages from an oracle deck or an Angel Messenger

You can learn to speak Angel language so that you don't need to seek assistance from an Angel Messenger.

Like anything, it takes practice, and some will have a more natural aptitude than others.

It's as much unlearning what you *think* intuition and Angel communication 'should' be, as it is learning.

It's actually more obvious and simpler than you think; once you begin to trust the messages, they increase.

Angel messages feel like love. They are a whisper, a quiet voice, a gentle loving reassurance, and a sudden wave of love that can sometimes bring you to tears.

With time and practice, everyone can do it. You've already done it!

Self-doubt is the biggest obstacle to overcome. The things that you dismiss as coincidences, or your imagination are most often the first whispers from your Angels.

If you find yourself wondering if something is a message or sign, then odds are it actually *is* a message.

Your signs and messages will be unique to you, have meaning only YOU understand, and are always best interpreted by you.

Your Angels are always with you.

Begin by asking for help. Do this in a journal, and when you receive an answer, write it in there also. Even if you're not sure. Write it anyway.

Over time, you will begin to develop your confidence and recognise YOUR Angels' messages. And you'll also have a wonderful record of all their lovely messages that you can look back on.

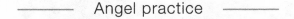

## Angel practice

Take out your Angel journal right now and ask your Angels for help with whatever is troubling you.

You might like to try some of the following questions:

- *Angels, please help me with* [describe your situation]. *What guidance do you have for me to help me with this situation?*
- *Angels, please show me what I can't see.*
- *Angels, what is my highest priority today to help me with my current experience?*

For intermediate to advanced Angel students, you might like to write out a full journal entry with your feelings about your current situation, then go through point by point and practise automatic writing, allowing your Angels to respond. Remember, Angels only speak with love, will never shame you, will never be angry, disappointed, or upset with you … this is how you begin to learn the difference between an Angel, and your ego.

**Angel Practice tip:** Angels speak first and softly, with a neutral tone of acceptance and love. Your ego speaks second, and loudly, and will bring in fear, shame, and self-doubt.

─────── Invocation ───────

*Angels, please help me hear your messages easily and clearly.*

**Guiding Angels:**
**Guardian Angels, Archangel Haniel, Archangel Faith**

# DAY 11

## Channelled Angel message

We want you to know that in order to hear our messages and feel our presence, you need to take a leap of faith. It requires trust.

We see that many of you have had your hearts broken previously, and that trust is hard for you.

We see that many of you have had difficult experiences with religion in the past, and we want you to know that we are not religion. Religion is a human construct. Love is not religion. Angels are not religion. We are love.

We see that some of you may have had a difficult experience with other Angel workers, who may not have honoured your experience or acted with integrity.

We also see that for many of you, Angels seem a fantastical

notion. One that has been used either for the religious, or for the 'new age' and alternative.

We want you to know that in order for you to live the life that you want, that you dream of, that you are manifesting, love is required. And to fully love requires taking a risk, opening your heart, and trusting.

We see that this is hard.

We want to help you learn to trust and to open your heart.

We want you to know that we are here to support all humanity now.

We want you to know that we are no more fantastical than a butterfly or a bumblebee! Just because you cannot see us with your physical eyes, does not mean we do not exist.

We want you to know that we will always offer guidance that is in your highest interest, and highest good.

We accept all parts of you, and will never shame you, talk down to you, or be mad or angry at you.

We understand the human experience and support and accept all aspects of it and will always guide you to your best-possible outcome.

All you need do is ask.

We are bound to respect your free will, so please do not forget to ask.

 Invocation

*Angels, please remind me to ask you for assistance, and to believe in myself, and trust the feelings and messages that I am receiving.*

**Guiding Angels:**
**Guardian Angels, Archangel Faith**

# DAY 12

*Channelled Angel message*

Every relationship has a purpose.

Your primary experience of love and being human in all its fullness comes through your relationships.

No one relationship is more important than another.

It is the experience of understanding yourself, of understanding another human, of learning about love, about pain, about joy, about grief, about forgiveness, about compassion, about betrayal, about ALL the multidimensional aspects of the richness of human life that is the point.

There are many rules on Earth.

They are not real. They are made up.

All that matters is following your own heart and being you.

Loving openly, being open to give love and receive love, is the point.

This is not limited to other humans. This extends to animals, to nature, and to the earth itself.

This year, many of you will begin to open your hearts.

The trigger may be grief or pain.

Or it may be a desire to experience deeper connections with family or a soul partner.

We would like to support you on this journey, and we urge you to be open to experiencing relationships with curiosity and wonder.

Miracles await you in the realm of your relationships.

Trust that everything is happening in divine timing. Focus on LOVE: loving all parts of your own life with fierce and passionate commitment.

Focus on loving all of those wonderful humans who are already in your life. On walking towards them with the intention of deepening your relationship and connection.

The loving relationship you seek comes from within your own heart.

We would love to support you on this journey.

──────── Invocation ────────

*Angels, please assist me to open more fully to give and receive love, in all areas of my life. Please help me first give love to myself.*

**Guiding Angels:**
**Archangel Chamuel, Archangel Zadkiel,**
**Archangel Raphael**

# DAY 13

*Channelled Angel message*

Religion is not our message.

We want more than anything right now to make this clear.

If you are religious, from any faith, we want you to know that you are always welcome with us. We love you.

If you are not religious, we want you to know that you are always welcome with us. We love you.

If you have experienced pain, confusion or hurt with religion, we honour your experience and we wish very much to help you heal that.

We understand that there are many who will say that you need to be religious to work with Angels. That is not true.

We also know that there are many of you who disagree with religion, and this may make you reluctant to work with us. We understand and we invite you to see for yourself.

Our messages are of love, compassion, and forgiveness. Of

course, we see this message is also central to most religious teachings.

We also want you to know that there is no intermediary required to work with us. There is no need to be in church or use a medium or priest.

We wish very much for you to remember that when you chose to incarnate on Earth, you were surrounded by and supported by a team of Angels, who agreed to guide you and be by your side for your every waking breath.

It is time for an awakening and remembering.

The love that we have for you is immense, and we see how isolated, lonely, and disconnected many of you feel right now.

As many of the structures and rules on Earth come into question and are dismantled, we wish to support you through this period of transition and uncertainty.

This period was foreseen and destined, and deep down you know that you chose to incarnate now.

It is indeed an incredible time and at times confusing to be alive.

However, you need not make this journey alone.

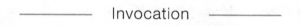 Invocation

*Angels, please help me see past any collective fears that have stemmed from my own experiences with religion, so that I may reclaim my sovereign connection with the divine.*

**Guiding Angels:**
**Archangel Michael, Archangel Uriel, Archangel Faith**

# DAY 14

## Angel lesson: Archangel Nathaniel

Archangel Nathaniel has youthful, playful, empowering, strong, and passionate energy and presence.

When his aura envelops you, you may notice that his energy holds both feminine and masculine tones in balance. He is passionate about empowering women or anyone experiencing a journey that is related to gender or sexuality and balancing our divine masculine and feminine energy.

Archangel Nathaniel assist us with authentic self-expression.

He is an Angel to call on when you are ready for a swift and complete transformation in your life.

He sees your true potential, and lovingly shows you the areas in your life that are holding you back from the happiness and joy that you seek.

Working with Archangel Nathaniel can be intense. He brings fire energy and will ask you to walk into your shadow healing at a fast pace.

Beliefs, patterns, habits, and relationships ALL come under the spotlight while working with Archangel Nathaniel.

Be prepared to let go and reinvent yourself over and over again when you begin the journey of working with Archangel Nathaniel.

He also has a playful and happy energy, so this process need not be serious and sombre! He will support you through a passionate exploration of all that you enjoy and love as a wonderful balance to shadow work and healing.

He is VERY present now as we move through times of collective fire, transformation and change energy.

I invite you to work with Archangel Nathaniel to support you through your own transformation.

*Archangel Nathaniel, I invite you to work with me. Please help me through the healing journey of peeling back my masks and coming into my authentic self.*

**Guiding Angel: Archangel Nathaniel**
**Energy: Masculine**
**Aura colour: Orange, yellow and red**

# DAY 15

## Channelled Angel message

We want you to know how proud we are of you. We are always here to remind you.

We accept and love you unconditionally.

We see every part of you and love you in a way that—if you fully opened to feel our presence—would bring you to tears.

There is nothing you have done, or can do, that will change our love for you.

We see every pain and challenge you have experienced, and we see how hard you are working to do your best.

We see you when you believe you are at your worst. We love you still.

We see you when you feel you have made a mistake. We want you to know that you have made no mistakes.

We see you when you experience joy and happiness.

We are always with you. We always love you. We are never disappointed in you. We are always proud of you.

We are right here, always, when you most need to feel our love and support, AND when you don't.

We hope you can feel less shame. We invite you to explore this concept. And we will love you when you do.

We hope you can feel less of a failure. And we will love you when you do.

We hope you can feel more compassion and softness towards yourself, and we can help you with this.

────────── Invocation ──────────

*Angels, please help me trust myself more on this journey. Please help me find compassion, forgiveness, and acceptance for myself.*

**Guiding Angels: Archangel Zadkiel, Archangel Jophiel**

# DAY 16

*Channelled Angel message*

We want you to know that imperfection, sadness, illness, heartbreak, and grief are all part of the human experience.

You have not done anything wrong.

These challenging and painful experiences are part of life, and every human experiences them.

You did not do something to deserve these challenges.

You need not compare your life to another's.

There is indeed a reason for *all* of life's challenges, even the ones that feel the most difficult.

You are never alone as you move through your darkest moments; in fact, that is when we are closest to you, and envelop you most in our love.

We wish to help you find some peace and acceptance with the layers of life, and find lightness, joy and even miracles in your most challenging experiences.

We assure you that everything will work out ok.

We also assure you that you are indeed strong enough to get through your current challenge.

──────── Invocation ────────

*Angels, please help me find peace with painful experiences. Please help me learn about love as I learn about pain.*

**Guiding Angels:**
**Archangel Azrael, Archangel Zadkiel, Archangel Michael**

# DAY 17

## Channelled Angel message

We want you to know that there is always guidance available to you; it's just not always what you expect or think you need to know.

When things feel overwhelming for you, when you don't know where to begin, we are here to guide you.

When there is a situation that is pressing for you, or causing you heartache, worry or stress, we are here to guide you.

There is always guidance available to you. However, it rarely is what you think you need to know!

Often, we see that you want to know the final destination, and when that will arrive.

However, the most helpful message for you often just reveals the next step on your journey towards that destination.

We wish to tell you that knowing the final result will not change things for you the way that you expect.

What will change things for you is finding peace in your present situation and accepting that everything is playing out exactly as it is supposed to and knowing that you are exactly where you are meant to be.

We can certainly guide you to your next step when you feel blocked or stuck.

And we can help you feel less afraid, less worried, less anxious, and less alone as you move through your current journey.

Truthfully, working with us will indeed change your life in ways that you cannot imagine right now.

This is surrender. This is faith. This is trusting in something bigger than yourself and relaxing into a journey that is beyond your control.

———— Invocation ————

*Angels, please help me find peace in trusting my journey.*
*Please help me let go, detach, and trust.*

**Guiding Angels:**
**Archangel Chamuel, Archangel Faith, Archangel Grace**

# DAY 18

*Channelled Angel message*

You are not meant to know when things will change, or the reason for an experience until after it has passed.

When we bring you guidance, via a medium or speaking with you directly, we show you options and pathways that you are not currently seeing.

We wish to remind you of the infinite possibilities and choices that exist for you. You have the ability to see these also.

We remind you to see things without filters of fear, doubt, shame, hurt, trauma, and unworthiness. Without attachment.

We invite you to feel the energy and emotions of all these possible choices, and to choose that which brings you the most joy!

We remind you that the choice is up to you and may be different to another's. There is no wrong choice.

We remind you that the future is never set in stone, that you have free will to choose at any point.

We remind you that knowing the result or outcome would in fact disempower you and take away from your experience.

We remind you that the experience is the point; it is why you are here, it is your whole purpose for being.

We remind you that the peace you seek from knowing the outcome is available to you right now, by making peace with not knowing.

We remind you that there is magic in the constant, ever-changing miracle of possibility. It is truly limitless! If you only knew how endless and immense the options are around you right now.

We invite you to begin a dialogue with us that is centred around 'show me what I do not see', rather than, 'tell me the outcome'.

Our goal is always to empower you.

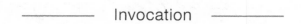 Invocation

*Angels, please show me what I can't see. Please remind me to look beyond my beliefs, walls, and veils. Please remind me to seek joy in any given moment.*

**Guiding Angels:**
**Archangel Faith, Archangel Jophiel, Archangel Haniel**

# DAY 19

*Channelled Angel message*

We want you to know that if you follow love in all things, your life will transform.

We want you to know that love, kindness, compassion, empathy, joy, passion, and all the things that feel like love, are your way forward.

Let this guide you in any situation you face.

Your heart always knows the answer to any dilemma.

It may take you some time to remember how to let it guide you, as you may have spent a lot of time learning to live in a way that is sensible, guarded, protected, and governed by your mind.

We can help you with this.

We invite you to be curious and look at situations with an open mind.

We invite you to notice your beliefs, and question whether they feel like they are serving you in your current situation.

We invite you to notice how your heart feels when you consider two different options for a situation.

We know that this journey may bring dramatic changes to your life, and that this may make you feel uncomfortable and even vulnerable.

We remind you that you want change, and that you feel dissatisfied currently.

We assure you that love will never lead you astray.

———————— Invocation ————————

*Angels, please help me soften and listen to my heart now.*

# DAY 20

## *Channelled Angel message*

We want you to know that time does not exist as you understand it.

There is always enough 'time'.

Everything will happen exactly when it is supposed to.

You will never run out of time.

All times, lives, ages and years exist right now.

You can bend time as you know it.

There is a huge amount that your current human awareness of time is yet to discover, and this is possible now.

The more you flex and stretch your awareness of the concept of time to expand to these ideas, the more space and time you will find opening up around you.

We invite you to notice where you feel stressed with your understanding of the time you have available to achieve your tasks, goals and dreams. Is this real? Is it true?

We invite you to notice where you make choices as a result of this belief. Do you sacrifice things that you wish to do because you believe you do not have enough time? Because you believe they are less important than other responsibilities in your life?

We invite you to notice that this is a belief and not a fact.

We invite you to practise awareness of the miraculous, magical energy of 'divine timing'. These words barely encompass the full alchemical magic and power of this concept.

It is ok to let go of any stress, fear, or anxiety over when things will happen in your life. We invite you to open your awareness to the idea of trusting that all that you desire is coming to you at the exact right moment.

Instead of attaching to when, we invite you to practise feeling. Close your eyes: how does it feel when you imagine your desire existing? When you imagine being in the home that you will own, when you imagine being in a relationship with your soul partner? We invite you to imagine this with every part of your heart so that it feels real to you in this moment.

We invite you to play with and explore this concept with curiosity!

————— Invocation —————

*Angels, please help me let go of linear time, and become aware of quantum time and infinite possibilities. Please help me expand into the infinite love of creation.*

**Guiding Angels:**
**Archangel Metatron, Archangel Ariel, Archangel Jeremiel**

# DAY 21

*Channelled Angel message*

We want you to know that death is not a final ending. It's a return home.

We would like to remind you that religion is not a part of our message.

We would like you to open your heart to the memory that exists within you of your eternal nature.

We remind you that you are part of something bigger than you have conscious awareness of. We know that deep down you believe or feel the truth of this.

Your conscious awareness returns home and transitions after

your physical Earth body dies.

You have indeed lived many times.

You are here now because you chose to be.

Your experiences are ones you chose and agreed to learn.

Your family and friends and all the people who are significant in your life, every single one of them—even the ones that you have had challenging experiences with—are in your life for a reason. Many of these people you have had multiple lifetimes with.

You experience love and forgiveness in a vastness that you cannot comprehend when you die and return home.

There is no 'Hell', judgement, or punishment as you understand these concepts.

There is family, infinite love, complete forgiveness and healing awaiting each and every one of you. Yes, each and every one of you.

True forgiveness, compassion, acceptance, and love heal you when you return, along with other healing processes that you need not understand now.

There is a consciousness that you understand as God, but God is not a religious being.

If you imagine creation force and love and awareness in one form, in a vastness that encompasses the universe, you are only grasping a fraction of this concept, this love that you call God.

We invite you to open your energy to the message today so that you may let go of some of the loneliness and fear of death that you experience.

———————— Invocation ————————

*Angels, please remind me that death is not the end.*
*Please remind me that I need not fear death.*

**Guiding Angels: Archangel Azrael, Archangel Michael**

# DAY 22

## Angel lesson: Archangel Michael

I don't see Angels with physical form or human features. I did when I first started. In my mind, I thought they were human, so I projected human form and features onto them. But Angels are not human. Angels are beings of light.

I see Angels in my mind as auras of radiant white, golden and coloured light. I feel their messages in my heart, and I see their aura colour in my mind. I don't see 'wings' as a bird has them, or as traditional images show. Rather, I see an immensity of the Angels' loving aura that is so big it almost feels like wings. Angels are a wave of love and light that is immense and can crack your heart into tears of joy when you first connect with them.

Angels respect our free will, love unconditionally, and serve all humanity.

They are not bound by the laws of time and space as we know them.

Archangels are different from Guardian Angels, and serve the collective, and have specific tasks or areas that they preside over.

Archangel Michael is often one of the first Archangels that people connect with. His vast energy is easy to connect with and is instantly calming and reassuring.

You do not need to be religious to work with Archangel Michael.

Archangel Michael has a primary mission to support all those who experience fear and anxiety. Archangel Michael can assist you to find a place where anxious feelings become a message that move through you and help you discover more about yourself and about life. Archangel Michael assures you that you are always safe, and that there is a lesson in every journey. Archangel Michael can help you learn to create stronger energetic and relational boundaries, and feel confident, brave, and powerful.

Working with Archangel Michael is more than just a temporary bubble of protection; it's a journey of empowerment to make peace with the discomfort and fear that comes from disconnection from divinity and disconnection from faith. It's a life-changing journey of self-discovery, rather than a band aid or temporary solution.

Archangel Michael also assists all lightworkers and starseeds on the journey of discovering and embodying their mission of service. He is the Angelic business coach, partner, and cheerleader you need, every step of the way.

When I began my own awakening journey, I chose to work with Archangel Michael morning and night, for two years.

Archangel Michael does not carry a sword. Swords are weapons, and Angels do no harm. He wields light, which is an expression of the infinite love of creation. His light cannot harm another. He works within the same boundaries and rules as all Angels. His light cannot be used without free will and permission.

 Invocation

*Archangel Michael, I invite you to work with me. I invite you to surround my aura in your protective energy and light so that I may focus on raising my vibration. Please show me how I may be of highest service.*

**Guiding Angel: Archangel Michael**
**Energy: Masculine**
**Aura colour: Indigo, purple, gold**

# DAY 23

## Channelled Angel message

There are no mistakes.

Everything is a learning experience.

There is no right or wrong. Every single human experience has value and meaning that you do not understand.

Not understanding is part of the experience. You will understand exactly when you are meant to.

The experience is the point.

Life can be very confusing and painful at times, but even during these difficult moments, it can also be joyful and filled with incredible grace and love.

We wish to remind you that one experience is not better than the other. They are both part of the plan, part of the miracle, part of the point and part of the reason you chose to experience life in human form.

Indeed, everything has a purpose, and there is a divine magic and interplay that is so vast and complex that if you could only understand how connected you are, and how significant even the most seemingly insignificant moments are, you would see miracles in every moment.

Nothing you do is wrong. Nothing is bad. Nothing is a mistake.

We want to help you remember the big picture of life and find some peace and ease in your experiences in the moment.

We remind you that we accept you unconditionally, and we encourage you to practise and seek unconditional acceptance of yourself.

———————— Invocation ————————

*Angels, please help me surrender and let go, so that I can allow myself to experience life with greater acceptance and compassion for myself and others.*

**Guiding Angels:**
**Archangel Zadkiel, Archangel Faith, Archangel Grace**

# DAY 24

## *Channelled Angel message*

Sometimes, for things to speed up, you need to slow down.

When things feel stagnant, blocked, or like you can't make any progress, we invite you to get curious, pause, and take notice of what's in front of you right now.

When you feel tired, lacking focus, or like 'time' is slipping away from you, we invite you to slow down, pause, recharge and listen.

When the energy around you is guiding you to slow and flow, and you are pushing and forcing, we ask you, how does that feel? Is it working? Is there another way?

The answers and breakthroughs you seek will come in their own time. Forcing them will not change this; in fact, it may delay it.

There is something here in the pause, in the space and quiet. If you push through, you may delay the message, the healing, the awareness or the perspective shift.

There is no deadline.

You will not miss out.

You will not run out of 'time'.

Notice that when you flow with the collective energy, it feels easier and more peaceful within you.

Notice that space and time open up around you once you let go of control, resistance and force.

You are exactly where you are meant to be. There is a message or experience here for you right now if you can settle into this current slow energy and open to receive it.

——————— Invocation ———————

*Angels, please help me let go of control, resistance, and attachment. Please show me what I can't see in this moment. Please show me my next step, and highest timeline.*

**Guiding Angels: Archangel Haniel, Archangel Faith**

# DAY 25

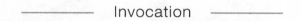

*Channelled Angel message*

Nothing is fixed. Everything is fluid.

Some days, you will radiate peace and calm, and feel one with the universal energy of all creation.

Other days, things will feel slow, stagnant, and heavy, and you will doubt your power to receive and to create the life you desire.

Both experiences are important and necessary for your human experience.

Both experiences teach you important awareness of yourself and your relationships.

You always have free will, and the truth of your ability to create and recreate is endless and extraordinary.

If you can open your energy to even just a fraction of a belief that change is possible, especially the most extraordinary and miraculous change, then energetic pathways around you begin to instantly activate and realign.

The future does not exist as a fixed state. The future is something that exists now, and is in constant flux, depending on your thoughts, actions, and feelings.

Let this be a message that helps you feel more peace in the present. As everything you desire is indeed possible, and that thought alone is enough to bring an energetic shift right now.

———————— Invocation ————————

*Angels, please help me find peace with the experience I am having right now in this moment, and open to the infinite possibilities available to me.*

**Guiding Angels:**
**Archangel Ariel, Archangel Metatron, Archangel Grace**

# DAY 26

## Channelled Angel message

We will guide you in ways that are unique and perfect for you.

We know your Angel language.

We know exactly what you need to hear, and when you need to hear it.

We also know when we need to let you experience finding the way yourself.

We know what information is in your highest good, and we will often answer your question with a redirection.

Sometimes we will not answer your specific question about 'when' something will change, because the experience would become void, and the experience is the point.

We see divinity in your situation and perfection in the timing, as we see the full picture that is as yet unrealised by you.

If we were to answer all your questions directly, it would disempower you, and in fact limit your experience.

We know your preferences and will bring you music when we know you most need to hear it, or love when you most need to feel it.

We will only show you the next step on your path that aligns with your highest good, rather than the outcome.

We can help you see other options available to you that are hidden, and a sense of how these might eventuate should you make that choice. But we also respect your free will and know you might choose an alternate path.

When you feel frustrated or blocked, we suggest you ask us 'What am I missing?' or 'What is my highest priority?' (Rather than 'When will this change?' or 'When will this occur?') and watch how things change with this shift in focus.

—————— Invocation ——————

*Angels, please show me my next step, my highest timeline, and my highest priority in this moment.*

**Guiding Angels:**
**Guardian Angels, Archangel Faith, Archangel Raziel**

# DAY 27

*Channelled Angel message*

We want you to know that everything will work out fine.

We want you to know that there is a reason for every seeming block, delay, redirection or pause.

We want you to know that you can soften into faith and know that the universe works to support you.

We want you to know that there is divine magic creating miracles in your life every second of every day.

We want you to know that the possibilities are explosive and endless around you, and that what seem like blocks are often redirections to a better outcome.

We want you to know that your potential in any given moment is limitless.

We want you to know that even though you may experience challenges, everything WILL work out fine, and there is a reason for everything. The reason is in the experience. The experience teaches you about love.

We want you to soften into this knowing, to experience more peace right now. The future will unfold as it's meant to.

———————  Invocation  ———————

*Angels, please help me let go and find peace in this moment.*
*Please help me break free of limiting beliefs about what is possible*
*for me.*

**Guiding Angels: Archangel Chamuel, Archangel Faith**

# DAY 28

*Angel lesson: Archangel Gersisa*

Archangel Gersisa cares for Earth on an energetic level.

She works with frequencies, grid lines and ley lines and is working to support all humans as they integrate and alchemise the new fifth-density (5D) energy. She also assists all starseeds who have agreed to anchor the new frequencies as part of their mission.

As the earth's frequency changes (which is happening now in waves that are compounding in frequency and intensity), you will notice that you may have a response, presenting as a physical, mental, or spiritual shift.

You may feel heavy, tired, and lethargic at times, or you may feel alive and energised and notice what feels like waves of energy moving through your body.

Part of this process will awaken and strengthen your energetic connection to the earth allowing energy from the earth to flow through your physical body and light body.

Archangel Gersisa wants to help you through this frequency shift, and any other times of intense energy and change. She asks you to remember that the earth is here to support you, not just physically but energetically.

She asks you to spend more time in nature, and in or by the bodies of water.

She asks you to take time to physically connect your body with the earth and the ocean. Take your shoes off, walk on the earth or swim in the ocean as often as you can in order to bring your physical and energetic body back into harmony and alignment with the changing Earth frequencies.

The more you can do this, the easier your adjustment to the frequency shifts will be.

If you notice that you feel out of sorts and cannot pinpoint the reason, take yourself to a sacred spot (somewhere sacred to you), and lie flat on the earth for as long as you are able, so that your body can process and align with the new frequency. Stay until you feel the process is complete for you.

It is important that you make this a regular practice now as the shifts are increasing in intensity and frequency.

You need not go through this shift alone.

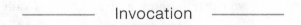

──────── Invocation ────────

*Archangel Gersisa, please remind me to allow myself to be*
*supported by the earth now. Please assist me to come into*

*frequency attunement with the earth, and to integrate new light*
*codes on all aspects of my mind, body, and spirit.*

**Guiding Angel: Archangel Gersisa**
**Energy: Feminine**
**Aura colour: Platinum/silver**

# DAY 29

## Channelled Angel message

We want you to know that you don't need to push anything.

We see that there is a common belief that you need to work hard, push through, and control your situation.

We want you to know that the opposite is the truth.

You do not need to push anything.

Every situation has a purpose, and there is no need to rush, force, resist or worry.

When things don't happen when you expect, or how you expect, we want you to know that this is perfect! What a relief, for had this happened now, you would have missed out on the perfect outcome and experience you are supposed to have.

We want to remind you that your understanding of what is possible is filtered and limited by your past experiences and beliefs. By your perception.

We want you to expand your awareness and open to the idea that there is divine timing and a perfect outcome in every situation. The outcome may not be what you expect, or when you expect, but it is exactly as it should be.

We remind you that pushing and forcing will only make your experience more uncomfortable and close you off to better possible outcomes.

Imagine now feeling a sense of faith and trust that the universe is guiding you towards your perfect outcome at the exact right time.

What if, by pushing now, you are delaying the process, and missing something miraculous?

When you feel the urge to push, force, resist or control, we invite you to be curious about what feels uncomfortable in this experience. The magic is here, in the not knowing, in the exploration and inquiry.

———————— Invocation ————————

*Angels, please help me find peace in the not knowing, and surrender and trust that all is as it should be.*

**Guiding Angels: Archangel Haniel, Archangel Faith**

# DAY 30

*Channelled Angel message*

There is no need to compare your journey to another. Ever.

Just because another person has succeeded in an area that challenges you means nothing about you, your worth, or your journey. Feel love for them for their success.

And equally, your life is no more difficult than another's. Every human has challenges that at times can seem insurmountable, and you never have the full picture from the outside looking in.

Your journey, your pace, your healing, your lessons, and growth have no relevance to any other human. They are the exact right experiences for you, at the exact right time.

You are exactly where you are meant to be. They are not better than you. You are equally not better than them.

Life is diverse, and its differences are to be celebrated and accepted.

We see your self-doubt and the fear and division it creates when you compare yourself to another, and we assure you that you are perfect in being you. No other could be you, and that is your gift.

Allow yourself to grow at the pace that works for you. Sometimes that will be fast. Sometimes that will be slow. Both are divine perfection.

Allow yourself to open your heart to joy for the success of those around you, as this will create an energy of success for yourself.

Practise cheerful loving joy for those who you would compare yourself to and know that you are in every way a divinely perfect human being.

There is nothing to fear from the success, joy, love, or beauty you see in another. These all exist in you also. There is enough space for you all to blossom and expand in your full divine radiance.

──────── Invocation ────────

*Angels, please help me see others as a mirror to my own potential and pathway. Please help me remember that there is no other, and that any judgement I cast to another, I cast to myself.*

**Guiding Angels: Archangel Zadkiel, Archangel Jophiel**

# DAY 31

*Channelled Angel message*

Religion is not what Angels are. Love is what Angels are.
We will repeat this message until it is known.

We serve and love all humanity.

You need not be religious to work with us.

We are love.

We have no part of organised religion as it is a construct of humanity that creates authority and control, both of which violate your free will. You do not need to be religious to work with us.

We accept religion as we accept and love all aspects of humanity.

However, we wish to clarify:

- You are a divine being.
- You are love itself.
- You need no intermediary to connect with us, with God, or with any expression of the divine.
- You need not seek a place of worship to connect with us or the divine. You are your temple.
- The divine exists in all things and in you, for you are not separate from the divine.
- Connecting with us is as easy as imagining what you want to say to us. We will hear you.

Connecting with us is simple and uncomplicated. It is feeling love and hoping. It is imagining and whispering. And we hear you and will whisper back in a way that you will easily learn to hear and understand.

———————— Invocation ————————

*Angels, please help me remember that I am one with the divine, and that I am worthy and able to have direct communication with Angels, God, and all divine expression. Please help me heal my relationship with God, Angels and the divine.*

# DAY 32

## Channelled Angel message

Everything is ok. All is exactly as it is supposed to be.

You have not done anything wrong. You have not made a mistake. Any discomfort or pain you feel right now has a reason that you do not understand yet.

We invite you to pause and take time to feel our loving assurance that all is ok.

There is nothing you need to do differently. You will find your way forward through your current experience at the exact right time.

It need not be any way other than exactly how it is right now.

You will know when things are meant to change. Until then, it's ok to not know. It's ok to trust. And please remember you are not alone and that we are always with you.

There is divine perfection in your situation right now. It is exactly the experience you need, and you are indeed divine perfection expressed.

───────── Invocation ─────────

*Angels, please help me find peace in this moment. Please help me trust that I am safe to let go and surrender to the path that is already presenting to me.*

**Guiding Angels: Archangel Faith, Archangel Chamuel**

# DAY 33

## Channelled Angel message

Everything you desire is possible.

The journey is the purpose, and every feeling, experience and roadblock on the way is a part of the plan.

You can feel your way through it, and we will support you.

We invite you not to give up on your dreams or the things that your heart calls for—especially the things that your heart calls for.

We invite you to explore the pain, sadness, hurt or fear. Your journey to all that you desire begins by walking inwards, into these feelings and into your heart.

Allow yourself to see and then express your feelings, pain, and fears. As you shine light on the darkness, you move closer towards your desires. The path of acceptance is faster than blocking your pain or keeping yourself safe.

———— Invocation ————

*Angels, please help me see, feel, and express any and all stored emotions in a way that I am ready for.*

**Guiding Angels:**
**Archangel Zadkiel, Archangel Michael, Archangel Raphael**

# DAY 34

## Channelled Angel message

We want you to know that you always have free will.

We want you to know that the future is not set in stone.

There are certain relationships and experiences that hold a strong likelihood or probability of occurring due to your soul contract chosen before incarnation. However, there is a fluidity and flexibility to everything, and you always have the freedom to choose a different pathway.

We want you to be aware of this so that you are aware of the limitless possibilities available to you.

There is a magic to destiny. It is as magic as the creation force itself. Everything is connected, and constantly moving.

Miracles are available in every breath you take.

One subtle shift of thought or a change in decision is enough to open new pathways around you and create a brand-new experience!

The future, past and present all exist now, in a fluid moving state.

You are never limited by what another predicts as your future.

No other can control your future by making a prediction. You always have the ability to choose another pathway.

Become discerning of stories that are presented as true, in any form, and choose not to give your power away to any external authority that states your future as true.

We want you to open to the fluidity of this aspect of our messages and to trust your heart and your own guidance. Your pathway, choices, and ability to create are magnificent and miraculous. You are divine love and a miracle in action, and you are always free.

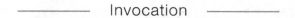

— Invocation —

*Angels, please help me strengthen my inner knowing, my intuition and my sense of truth as it appears for me. Please help me practise discernment and boundaries.*

**Guiding Angels: Archangel Michael, Archangel Haniel**

# DAY 35

*Channelled Angel message*

We want you to know that it is safe to open your heart to love.

We want you to know that this is your most important next step.

We want you to know that protecting yourself from hurt will also protect yourself from feeling love. It will filter and block the amount of love that you are able to both give and receive. And this will impact all your relationships, including your relationship with yourself.

We want you to know that it's ok, that you have done the best you can. You have not made a mistake or done the wrong thing by protecting your heart.

We want you to know that you are now ready to begin to open your heart, and that we will support you through this process.

We want you to know that this is for everyone, regardless of whether you are in a love relationship or not. For this is a process that is happening for all humans right now.

We want you to know that the feelings you have been having and the messages you have been receiving about opening to deeper connections and deeper love in your life are true and real.

We want you to know that the physical sensations that you have felt in your heart chakra are a natural part of the process.

We want you to know that you may experience physical and emotional releases as you open your heart, as you let go of stored pain, and as you remember what it is like to *feel* more. You will adjust and acclimatise to the intensity of feelings, and there is no danger. This is what it feels like to be open hearted, and it is your natural state.

We invite you to open to our love, and to allow us to support you gently through this process.

You are ready.

*Angels, please help me gently open my heart to give and receive love. Please help me soften, open, and let down any walls and barriers that no longer serve me.*

**Guiding Angels:**
**Archangel Zadkiel, Archangel Chamuel, Archangel Raphael**

# DAY 36

*Channelled Angel message*

We want you to know that love is the reason for all things.

All your experiences are to teach you about love.

Love is the force that created you and creates all things. Love is all around you in a multitude of miraculous expressions, and we remind you that you are one of those divine, perfect expressions of love!

You are love. We are love. And we love you!

We want you to know that when things feel difficult, the answer is always found in love.

We invite you to slowly become curious about where love is present or absent in your life.

We invite you to notice where you are protecting yourself from pain and hurt, as this also creates a barrier to love.

We invite you to notice the things that open your heart and fill you with radiant love, and to allow more of this in your life!

We invite you to notice that feeling of heart-stretching, heart-expanding, joyful, blissful love, and know that this is available to you every day.

We invite you to spend time in nature or with animals, as this will help you open more quickly to love.

We invite you to trust that you are safe and protected, and that nothing negative can come from loving more, opening more to love, or giving more love!

We invite you to feel your heart opening now, and we love you so much!

<hr>

## Invocation

*Angels, please help me gently open my heart so that I may give and receive more love.*

**Guiding Angels:**
**Archangel Chamuel, Archangel Michael, Archangel Raphael**

# DAY 37

*Channelled Angel message*

We want you to know that you are infinitely loveable.

There is nothing you need to do, change or be for you to be loved.

You are a radiant being made entirely from and of love.

We love you more than you can comprehend! You come from love and will return to love!

Those fleeting blissful moments where you feel your heart crack open to intense joyful love are a mere fraction of the love we feel for you, the love inside you, and the love available to you!

We want you to remember that everything about you is loveable, for you are love!

We want you to practise opening your heart to these feelings of love as we surround you with our loving energy and remind you of your divine right to feel this.

We want to support you to begin by practising loving yourself more and allowing yourself to receive love from us. As you practise receiving love from the divine, you will find it easier to receive love from those you care about in your life.

The more you open your heart to this feeling, the more you will adjust to the intensity of this love that we are washing through you. And the more love and joy you will notice in all areas of your life.

──────── Invocation ────────

*Angels, please help me become more comfortable giving and receiving love, beginning with your love.*

**Guiding Angels: Archangel Jophiel, Archangel Chamuel**

# DAY 38

*Angel lesson: Archangel Chamuel*

Archangel Chamuel can assist you to open your heart to experience more love in your life.

The first step is to turn inwards and begin a deep exploration of loving yourself. He invites you to work with him to begin a process of deep, immersive, rebellious self-love.

He invites you to begin healing places where you have avoided love, to unlock your heart chakra to give and receive more love, and to remember that you are infinitely loveable.

This journey is slow, and gentle. It will also encompass other core themes that are central to Archangel Chamuel's message: finding more internal peace on a day-to-day basis, finding your soulmate if that is your next journey, healing soul family relationships, opening your heart to the love of the divine and your Angels, and living with love as your guiding light.

If you feel guided to this journey, you will notice that your heart chakra feels warm and filled with positive soft energy as you connect to this message.

He wants you to know that you are ready and worthy, and that he can help you adjust and acclimatise to this gradual heart-opening process, and to heal any blocks, pains or hurts that come up as you open your tender heart.

You are safe to love. You are love. He loves you. This journey is vital to your larger life experience and purpose right now, and the most important next step for you to take.

It is not solely about finding a soulmate, though that may well be a consequence of this journey. It is more about reconnecting your heart to the divine and recalling how to live from and with love.

———————— Invocation ————————

*Archangel Chamuel, I invite you to work with me now. Please assist me as I explore love in all ways that support me to open to giving and receiving love.*

**Guiding Angel: Archangel Chamuel**
**Energy: Masculine**
**Aura colour: Pale green**

# DAY 39

*Channelled Angel message*

We want you to know that death is not the end.

We want you to know that death is a transition.

We want you to know that we are with you, as you grieve a loved one.

We want you to know that love exists in a magnitude so big that your beautiful heart cannot even imagine it, and that this is where you return to.

We want you to know that Heaven, as you understand it, exists (although without many of the rules that have been written).

We want you to know that all is forgiven, all are welcomed back with love. There is no discrimination, no requirements, no separation, no judgement, and no rules. All are welcomed. All are loved.

We want you to know that you will see your loved one again, in a different form.

We want you to know that you will go on, also. You are indeed eternal.

We want you to know that grief is a part of the process, and that we can help you with this. Grief is an expression of love. It is safe and necessary to express it.

We want you to know that there is light in death as well as darkness.

We want you to know that love is the way through this journey when it comes into your life, and that we are with you to support you.

## Invocation

*Angels, please assist me now when I most need it, as I navigate my own fears of death, or the death of someone I love. Please help me process the pain and grief now and feel your loving support in my darkest hour.*

**Guiding Angels: Archangel Azrael, Archangel Michael**

# DAY 40

*Angel lesson: Signs*

Receiving signs and messages from the Angels is not as hard as you think.

In fact, most of the time, they make it as easy as possible for you.

Angels know you. They love you and they want to hear from you.

Angels know if you are musical and will send you songs that have instant meaning. You might turn on the radio and the first song you hear stops you in your tracks. You might hear the same song on repeat for days. Or you might wake up with a song in your head (if so, go and check the lyrics).

Angels know if you like to receive things visually, so they send you images or visual signs in books, on the internet or literally in signs in your day-to-day life.

Angels know if you need to hear a message, so they send a stranger or friend to pass on just what you need to hear.

Angels know if nature and animals are your thing, so they send butterflies, rainbows, ladybugs, or other meaningful animals or natural experiences.

How do you know if it's a sign or message from the Angels? When something slaps you in the face and takes your breath away. When you immediately wonder if it's a coincidence, if you're imagining it, or if you're making it up. When you wonder, *Is this a sign?*

It's a sign.

It really is that simple.

The hardest part is trusting that it's a sign. And with practice, that will become easier and easier.

The more you trust, the easier it gets, and the more messages you will get.

As you become more confident recognising the signs, you will feel guided to learn how to communicate with the Angels on a deeper level.

Everyone can learn to speak with Angels!

―――――― Invocation ――――――

*Angels, please help me receive your messages in ways that are easy for me to recognise. Please help me have faith and trust the signs I receive.*

**Guiding Angels:**
**Archangel Raziel, Archangel Haniel, Archangel Faith**

# DAY 41

## Angel lesson: Guardian Angels

You have Guardian Angels who are with you your whole life.

Every single human has Guardian Angels.

Your main Guardian Angel is with you every second of the day. They will often have a very similar temperament, personality, and energy to you, as one of the central purposes of a Guardian Angel is to mirror your highest potential.

Guardian Angels are different to spirit guides, who have human energy.

Guardian Angels will never laugh at you, tease you, shame you, belittle you, or be unforgiving or unkind in any way.

Guardian Angels have a different energy and purpose to Archangels. They are closer to earth, so have a more accessible energy. Archangels have a 'bigger', more universal energy, and exist at a higher plane.

Guardian Angels focus specifically on your life and growth. They can show you options that exist to you in a situation or life path, and help you feel into which ones are for your highest good.

They help you look at the big picture of a situation and keep you on track for the long-term journey.

They are always proud, accepting and loving towards you.

You can tell the difference between Guardian Angel energy and human energy, as they speak with you without any attachment to your decisions, and with a wave of love that is bigger than anything you've felt from any relationship you've experienced.

You will feel some sort of internal recognition and inner truth when you first connect with your main Guardian Angel, which always happens exactly when it is supposed to.

Guardian Angels have a golden aura, and often appear behind either shoulder, in a guarding position. It is common for some starseeds to have two, three or even four Guardian Angels.

Guardian Angels don't mind if you don't know their names. They aren't attached to names at all and are often lovingly amused when we hold attachment to receiving their name. Remember, they don't have a physical body, and no need to use a sound vibration to communicate with each other, or you.

Over time, you can practise learning how the different Angel energies feel. And this will help you distinguish between human/ spirit, Guardian Angel, and Archangel energy. And of course, the types of guidance and messages you receive from all three are different too.

———————— Invocation ————————

*Guardian Angels, please present yourselves to me now in a way that is easy for me to recognise your energy, guidance, and love.*

**Guiding Angels: Guardian Angels**

# DAY 42

## Channelled Angel message

There are many changes happening on Earth right now. This is something we can help you with.

We are coming through now with new messages and new energy to assist you through a time of great personal and collective change.

The energy of Earth is changing.

There is change happening at a rapid rate all around you.

You are experiencing rapid personal growth, healing, and expansion in all areas of your life.

For some time now, there has been a speed and intensity to this process that has felt uncomfortable and palpable.

And there are also opportunities, miracles, healing, and personal transformation available to you like never before.

We wish to assist you with this process.

We wish to make the journey feel less intense, less isolating, and less challenging.

We wish to offer you support, love, compassion, guidance, and acceptance through this period of change.

We wish to help you heal, find your purpose, let go, and create more meaning, joy and happiness in your life.

We wish to assist you through the darkest times, so that you may find miracles and love even in the depths of the hardest challenges.

We wish to assist you to acclimatise to the intensity of the new Earth energy and find new ways to be that are more helpful in the current climate.

Most of all, we wish for you to feel loved.

*Angels, please assist me to open to the infinite energy of all creation now. Please help me through new light-code activations and the expansion and integration of new energy. Please assist me to find peace through my awakening and ascension process.*

**Guiding Angels:**
**Archangel Metatron, Archangel Gersisa, Archangel Haniel**

# DAY 43

## Angel lesson: Archangel Azrael

Archangel Azrael helps with everything to do with death, dying and our return to the light.

The Angels want you to know that you do not have to navigate this area alone, and that Archangel Azrael can assist with all aspects that you find challenging.

Archangel Azrael has a male energy, and a cream and pure-white aura.

His energy is incredibly calming and comforting. Working with him will ease heartache, grief, fear and worry about death.

Archangel Azrael assists at the time of death and oversees and guides the transition process.

You can ask him for guidance before and after the loss of a loved one.

He assists in hospitals and with all those who work to support the death process.

He can send in helpers in the form of friends, family, and strangers to ease your process when you need it.

He can assist and help with mediumship, past-life healing, past and future timeline balancing, and generational healing.

He assists with helping all souls cross to the light, including lost or stuck souls.

He wishes us to know that death is not something to be feared, that it is a sacred part of the human process just as birth is, and that it is another profound experience of love.

He wishes us to know that the transition process is beautiful, filled with white light and love, and deeply healing for all souls.

He wishes us to know that all souls return to the same place, that there is no good or bad place, and that all are forgiven. It is just love. All come from it and all return to it.

He wishes us to know that all pain is healed.

He wishes us to know that the pain of the loss of a loved one is sacred and filled with love, and he wishes us to find some acceptance with this process.

Most of all, he wishes us to feel some comfort with the knowledge that we are indeed eternal. That you will continue, and that you will see your loved ones again in a different place and a different form.

He sends a huge wave of love to you right now if you need it.

## Invocation

*Archangel Azrael, please assist me to find grace, peace and love in the experience of death. Please help me release my fears about death.*

**Guiding Angel: Archangel Azrael**
**Energy: Masculine**
**Aura colour: Cream & white**

# DAY 44

## Channelled Angel message

Nothing is truly bad. It is all part of the miracle of life.

We want you to know that you are not doing anything wrong when things don't feel happy or positive all the time in your life.

We want you to know that you have not done something to deserve a difficult situation.

We want you to know that life is meant to be all shades of the human experience.

We want you to know that nobody escapes difficult challenges. Everyone is here to learn. Everyone faces challenges and everyone experiences pain.

We want you to know that these challenges are here to teach you something, and that the experience may end up being something life changing and miraculously positive for you, after some time has passed.

We want you to know that even the most difficult and challenging of human experiences can be filled with incredible grace and love.

We want you to open to this idea, so that you don't fight so hard to avoid pain.

We want you to soften into an awareness that pain is part of your experience, and not necessarily a negative part.

We want you to know that even when things are hard, we are with you, and especially when things feel hard, we are with you.

We want you to become curious when things feel challenging or painful, and ask for guidance now more than ever, as there is always a pathway forward, and we want nothing more than to assist you.

Nothing is truly bad. Every experience is valuable in its own right, and you will be ok.

*Angels, please help me find acceptance with the most painful and difficult challenges in my life. Please help me feel the pain and see my pathway forward.*

**Guiding Angels:**
**Guardian Angels, Archangel Faith, Archangel Michael**

# DAY 45

## Channelled Angel message

We want you to know that love is the answer to everything.

We want you to know that you can never make a mistake in love.

We want you to know that the purpose of life is to love and be loved, and everything you experience connects to this in some way.

We want you to know that every obstacle you face, every challenge, every roadblock or painful experience, can be made easier or resolved with love as your guide.

We want you to know that things often feel harder if you close yourself off to love.

We want you to know that this principle applies to every area of your life, not just relationships. We especially want you to know that it applies most importantly to yourself.

We want you to know that loving yourself is the single most important thing you can do. We want you to know that the more you love yourself, the more your life will transform in wonderful, seemingly miraculous ways!

We want you to know that loving your life—and choosing to fully express yourself with activities, people and choices that are motivated by your passions, by the things you love—is essential.

We want you to know that any decision you need to make can be answered by your heart.

We want you to know that learning to live this way will take practice and at times conscious rebellion. But the rewards will be tremendous and life altering.

—————— Invocation ——————

*Angels, please show me the pathway that feels like love. Please help me love myself, my life, and my loved ones more. Please help me soften and open to love.*

**Guiding Angels: Archangel Chamuel, Archangel Jophiel**

# DAY 46

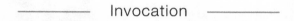
*Channelled Angel message*

We wish you could see the energy of possibility all around you!

What we see around you, in your energy field, is endless and infinite.

There are so many options available to you, and these are swirling with the magical energy of creation and miracles!

Nothing is fixed.

Everything is possible.

Your ability to choose is vast and limitless.

These possibilities swirl around you, interacting with people and situations.

It is so dynamic, ever changing.

You never miss a possibility.

You never make a mistake.

The complexity and synchronicity of this truth is so wonderful that we wish you to open to it.

Everything is happening with a divine magical order that is perfection.

Options that you cannot fathom exist right now.

Your imagination is the gateway, as is your ability to feel, give and receive love.

───────────  Invocation  ───────────

*Angels, please help me awaken to the infinite possibility*
*of divine love.*

**Guiding Angels: Archangel Ariel, Archangel Chamuel**

# DAY 47

*Channelled Angel message*

We want you to know that pain is a gateway to healing, to love and to enlightenment.

We want you to understand more about the message that everything happens for a reason.

We want you to understand more about the experience of pain and suffering.

We want you to understand more about the depth of the human experience.

We want you to understand that painful experiences will always be a part of the human journey, until universal consciousness is reached.

We want you to understand that whilst there are negative actions by people in life that do cause pain and suffering, it is still possible to experience miracles, love, and healing from this journey.

We want you to know that the goal of life is not to remove suffering and pain or to have a trauma-free life. Every human experiences pain and suffering.

We want you to know that pain and suffering are just the beginning, and that this is where your learning begins. A positive outcome can indeed follow a painful experience. Forgiveness and love can be found in the darkest depths of pain. Grace exists in the places you least expect it.

We invite you to begin to open to the journey of faith.

We understand that this is a challenge, and we want to support you.

We want you to know that just because you experience painful events in your life does not mean you are unlovable, unlucky, unsuccessful, or unloved by the divine.

Become curious about the pathway present in your darkest moments, for there is always a pathway. Become curious about finding love and light on your healing journey. Become curious about your connection to the divine. This is where your miracles will occur.

Your miracle may be that you find love in darkness, or that you find forgiveness. Perhaps you find your purpose. Or it may be far greater than that ... it may be that you experience a deep, miraculous healing.

## Invocation

*Angels, please help me let go and trust the journey that is unfolding right now in my life. Please help me see the next step, and open to miracles now.*

**Guiding Angels: Archangel Faith, Archangel Zadkiel**

# DAY 48

## Channelled Angel message

On the days when you cannot feel us and need us most, take yourself to nature.

We are always with you.

Some days, your energy will be open and radiate light, and you will feel and hear us easily.

Some days, particularly on challenging days, your energy will be focused on your survival, and it will seem much harder to hear our loving guidance.

On these days, we urge you to go to nature.

When things feel the hardest for you, when you feel exhausted or sad, or are experiencing pain or deep suffering, nature will help you in ways you cannot imagine.

The healing power of nature is magnificent and infinite.

Nature brings you the reminder that you are indeed a miracle in form, and that further miracles are possible.

The energy and vibration of nature is such that it automatically clears and begins to heal your aura and energy field, and your physical body.

The longer you spend in nature, the more healing you will experience.

You will automatically be drawn to certain places in nature that you sense are power points of healing energy. Trust this. They are indeed powerful healing points. Whilst these exist everywhere, certain ones will call to your energy as a match to what you need to experience right now.

You are no different from the trees, the oceans, the sky.

You are no different from the animals, the birds and the bees.

In nature, you will recall this truth, and the simplicity of this miraculous fact will help create a peace within you when you are troubled.

You will find your oneness in nature under the trees, by the seashore, on the banks of the rivers and in the rainforest.

Follow any guidance you receive to be in nature. For it is us whispering to you, offering healing and wisdom.

<hr />

## Invocation

*Angels, please remind me that I am nature, and that nature is me. Please remind me to take myself to nature so that I can begin my healing and awakening journey with the loving support of all plants and animals, and the earth beneath my feet.*

**Guiding Angels: Archangel Ariel, Archangel Gersisa**

# DAY 49

Channelled Angel message

Whatever challenge you have, we can guide you. Just ask.

We can see possibilities and options available to you that you can't.

We see your highest pathway.

We love you SO much, and we want nothing more than to assist you when you are finding life difficult.

We are always with you, and we want you to have faith in our guidance.

We know that it seems hard to speak with Angels, but it's not really. It's very simple, and you can learn. It just takes some practice. And some faith.

We will never interfere with your free will.

We will never give you negative, fear based, shameful or scary messages.

We will always guide you with love.

We are so proud of you!

We will often show you the next step and help you in ways that you do not even realise exist.

We may redirect your focus elsewhere in order to solve a problem. Or we may place a solution in your path in the form of a message, or guidance from a friend or stranger.

All you have to do is ask.

We are always listening! Our answers will come to you in the exact right way at the exact right time.

It really is a dialogue of faith.

———————— Invocation ————————

*Angels, please help me remember to ask for guidance by giving me gentle reminders of your love and presence.*

**Guiding Angels: Guardian Angels**

# DAY 50

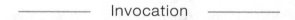
*Channelled Angel message*

We are so happy that you are opening to work with us!

Can you feel our joy? The love we feel for you is immense. And to see you begin to take a leap of faith and trust yourself, and trust us, makes us feel joy beyond belief.

We see that you are having an experience as you begin to open to us.

We see that you are beginning to trust the messages you are receiving.

We see that you are beginning to identify what feels like truth to you. This makes us very happy!